YOUR KNOWLEDGE HAS VALUE

- We will publish your bachelor's and master's thesis, essays and papers

- Your own eBook and book - sold worldwide in all relevant shops

- Earn money with each sale

Upload your text at www.GRIN.com
and publish for free

The E-Fulfillment Process 2020 of Amazon

GRIN 😃

Bibliographic information published by the German National Library:

The German National Library lists this publication in the National Bibliography; detailed bibliographic data are available on the Internet at http://dnb.dnb.de.

ISBN: 9783346264060
This book is also available as an ebook.

© GRIN Publishing GmbH
Nymphenburger Straße 86
80636 München

Print and binding: Books on Demand GmbH, Norderstedt, Germany
Printed on acid-free paper from responsible sources.

The present work has been carefully prepared. Nevertheless, authors and publishers do not incur liability for the correctness of information, notes, links and advice as well as any printing errors.

GRIN web shop: https://www.hausarbeiten.de/document/935496

The E-Fulfillment Process in Electronic Commerce

Summer Semester 2020

Scientific Essay

Bachelor of Science (B.Sc.)

Information Systems - Business Information

Systems

FOM University of Applied Sciences for Economics and

Management

Remagen, May, 29th, 2020.

Table of Contents

List of Figures III

1. Introduction .... - 1 -

1.1. Motivation and Aim .... - 1 -

1.2. Defining an E-Marketplace in E-Commerce .... - 1 -

1.3. The Relevance and Meaning of E-Fulfillment .... - 2 -

2. The Four Phases of Transactions and their Manifestation in the E-Fulfillment process .... - 2 -

2.1. Phase 1: Gathering Information – eSearch and eOffer Process .... - 3 -

2.1.1. The eSearch Process .... - 3 -

2.1.2. The E-Offer Process .... - 4 -

2.2. Phase 2: Reaching an Agreement - The eMatching Process .... - 5 -

2.2.1. Online-Catalog-Process .... - 6 -

2.2.2. Online-Request-Process .... - 7 -

2.2.3. Online-Auction-Process .... - 8 -

2.2.3.1. The Forward-Auction .... - 8 -

2.2.3.2. The Reverse-Auction .... - 8 -

2.3. Phase 3: Completing the Transaction – The eTransaction Process .... - 9 -

2.4. Phase 4: After Sales Service – The After-e-Sales Process .... - 10 -

2.4.1. Returns-Management .... - 11 -

2.4.2. Repurchase-Service .... - 12 -

3. Conclusion .... - 12 -

Bibliography IV

List of Figures

Figure 1. Basic Relationships on an Electronic Marketplace…………………………………- 1 -

Figure 2. Transaction Process on an E-Marketplace…………………………………………- 2 -

Figure 3. Amazon On-Site Search Bar and Departments……………………………………..- 4 -

Figure 4. Data Normalization for the Product-Catalog………………………………………- 5 -

Figure 5. Selection of Fixed Pricing- and Product Variants on a Single Catalog-Offer………...- 6 -

Figure 6. The Broad Selection of Services and Products on Craigslist…………………………- 7 -

Figure 7. Reverse Auction: Providers are Lowering the Price………………………………….- 9 -

Figure 8. User View of the Payment Process on Amazon…………………………………...- 10 -

Figure 9. The two Possible Routes for the After-e-Sales Process………………..……..……..- 11 -

1. Introduction

1.1. Motivation and Aim

This essay aims to define and explain the comprehensive e-fulfillment process in detail as well as its essential existence within e-marketplaces. The series of sub-processes making up the e-fulfillment process will be presented in the corresponding order of the four phases of transaction. Of all five sub-processes the e-matching process will be covered in further detail.

1.2. Defining an E-Marketplace in E-Commerce

"An e-marketplace (also called e-market, virtual market, or marketspace) is an electronic space where sellers and buyers meet and conduct different types of transactions."[1]. Taking this definition as a reference one can say that an e-marketplace serves as one of the possible platforms for transactions between providers and demanders in electronic-commerce[2] [3]. E-marketplaces differ in their strategy and layout and are composed of a variety of specifications such as branch specificity (vertical- and horizontal marketplaces)[4], different pricing models such as e-auctions, dynamic- and fixed pricing[5] as well as a selection of possible operator models (e.g. B2B, B2C, C2C)[6] [7].

Figure 2. Basic Relationships on an Electronic Marketplace

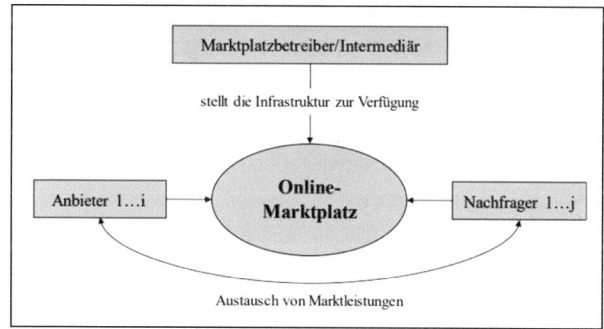

Source: Turban; E., Whiteside; J., King; D., Outland, J., Introduction to Electronic Commerce and Social Commerce, 2017, P. 32..

---

1 Turban; E., Outland; J., King; D,. Lee; J. K., Liang; T-P., Turban; D.,Electronic Commerce 2018, 2018, P. 39.
2 Cf: Teuteberg; F., E-Marketplace-Modelle, 2019, PP. 2-3.
3 Cf: Turban; E., Whiteside; J., King; D., Outland, J., Introduction to Electronic Commerce and Social Commerce, 2017, P. 6.
4 Cf: Deges; F., Grundlagen des E-Commerce, 2020, P. 51.
5 Cf: Turban; E., Outland; J., King; D,. Lee; J. K., Liang; T-P., Turban; D., Electronic Commerce 2018, 2018, P. 54.
6 Cf: Olbrich; R., Schultz; C., Holsing; C., Electronic Commerce und Online-Markteting, 2019, PP.33-34.
7 Cf: Wirtz; B., Digital Business Models, 2019, P. 165.

1.3. The Relevance and Meaning of E-Fulfillment

The term e-fulfillment is not always defined with equal means in literature. One of the key inconsistencies by definition is the overall relevance of the process for all marketplace sub-processes. Taking multiple definitions into consideration I will align myself with the definition from Kollmann[8], Shütte[9], Monero[10] and Olbrich[11] of the e-fulfillment process as an overarching process covering all marketplace-related sub-processes that - in combination - make up the entire operational procedure and logistics of completing a transaction between providers and demanders:

Figure 2. Transaction Process on an E-Marketplace.

Source: Kollmann; T., E-Business, 2019, P. 543.

2. The Four Phases of Transactions and their Manifestation in the E-Fulfillment process

As can be drawn from the above diagram, a transaction on an e-marketplace basically proceeds in four stages. Each of these phases are accompanied by the e-fulfillment process and each of the individual sub-processes are described in the following.

8 Cf: Kollmann; T., E-Business, 2019, PP. 559-560.
9 Cf: Schütte; R., E-Fulfillment, 2018, PP. 3-4.
10 Cf: Monero; M., Payaro., A., Implementation of e-procurement and e-fulfillment processes:A comparison of cases in the motorcycle industry, 2004, P. 342.
11 Cf: Olbrich; R., Schultz; C., Holsing; C., Electronic Commerce und Online-Markteting, 2019, PP. 36-37.

2.1. Phase 1: Gathering Information – eSearch and eOffer Process

A mandatory prerequisite for any successful transaction is the encounter of demand and supply. If a customer is unable to navigate through the large database on an e-marketplace or even find a suitable marketplace for his product in the first place, he is most certainly not going to enter the next phase of transaction. The same problem exists for the marketplace-providers as they are not visible for their target groups if they cannot provide adequate data about their products and services.

2.1.1. The eSearch Process

As can be derived from its name, the e-search process enables a visitor of the e-marketplace to search specifically for his product within the e-marketplace database. It is however important to separate between the on-site e-search process and the off-site e-search process:

The term off-site e-search-process describes the prior searching process for a suitable place of procurement[12]. In this prior step, a customer would usually type his desired item into a browser-based search engine such as www.google.com to be then directed to price comparison portals (e.g. Google Shopping) and a selection of marketplaces that include the sought item in their product catalog[13].

The on-site searching process can then be a personalized interaction between e-marketplace and customer in which the user can navigate through the product catalog (located in the data warehouse database) in detail and filter out offerings that match his search term, optionally receiving personal suggestions in the process[14]. The buyer may achieve this by selecting filters or formulating search queries matching the product name. An example of this on-site e-search process would be the utilization of Amazons search bar or department selection:

---

12 Cf: Kollmann; T., E-Business, 2019, P. 302.
13 Cf: Turban; E., Outland; J., King; D,. Lee; J. K., Liang; T-P., Turban; D., Electronic Commerce 2018, 2018, PP. 44-45.
14 Cf: Turban; E., Outland; J., King; D,. Lee; J. K., Liang; T-P., Turban; D., Electronic Commerce 2018, 2018, PP. 44-45.

Figure 3. Amazon On-Site Search Bar and Departments.

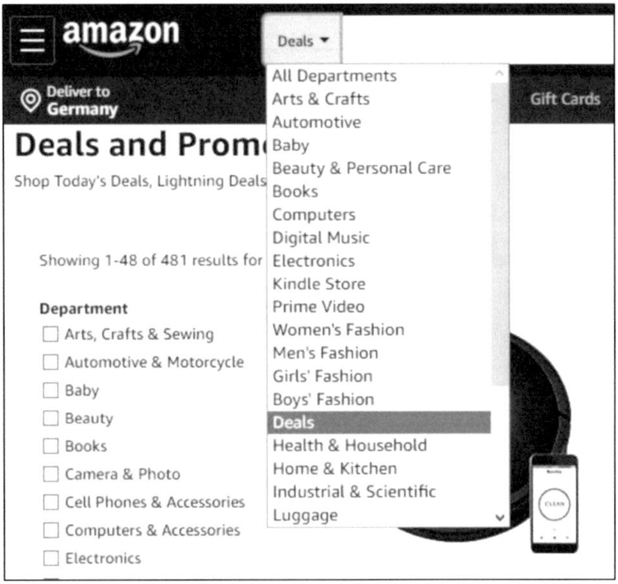

Source: Self-made screenshot from the website www.amazon.de.

2.1.2. The E-Offer Process

The e-offer process in itself consists of may sub-processes and services that enable providers to list information on their products and about themselves in the marketplace product catalog[15]. The marketplace-owner defines both format and type of information-exchange which terminates in the (often ERP-driven) integration of new offers into the marketplace database[16]. A direct data-integration is however rarely possible and a previous "Cleansing"[17] step before the data is stored in the database is necessary, as many providers operate with own formats for their offer-description:

---

15 Cf: Kollmann; T., E-Business, 2019, P. 544.
16 Cf: Nenninger; M., Lawrenz; O., B2B-Erfolg durch eMarkets und eProcurement, 2002, P. 77.
17 Nenninger; M., Lawrenz; O., B2B-Erfolg durch eMarkets und eProcurement, 2002, P. 81.

Figure 4. Data Normalization for the Product-Catalog.

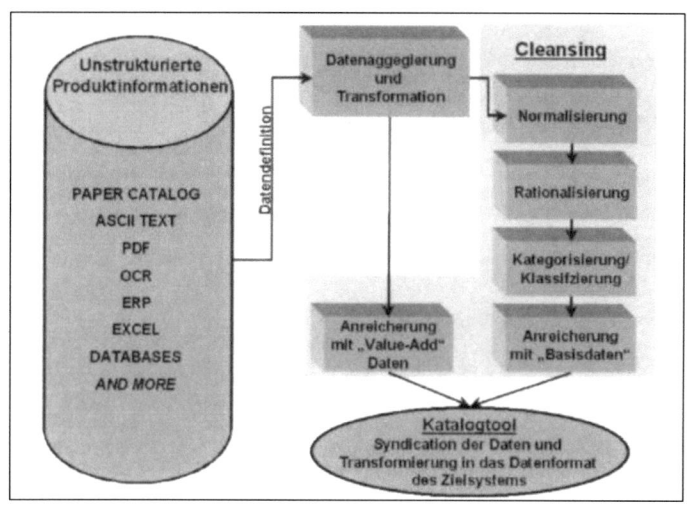

Source: Nenninger; M., Lawrenz; O., B2B-Erfolg durch eMarkets und eProcurement, 2002, P. 81.

"Content is King"[18] and it is often underestimated by many e-marketplace providers how important a diverse but structured representation of offerings on the e-marketplace website is.

2.2. Phase 2: Reaching an Agreement - The E-Matching Process

Any transaction that got conducted in a legal manner has to be verifiable in a contract. The previous terms and details of such a contract (including all transaction-specific details) on an e-marketplace are determined in the e-matching process.

In literature the e-matching process can be defined as the next step in matching supply and demand between provider and customer, that (when an agreement on all product and exchange related conditions was found) will lead into the closure of a legal contract between both parties[19] [20] [21]. Matching in its most basic form means the equality of two data sets. The customers search request will hence be evaluated in a way that it matches to a selection of specific offers on the e-marketplace database[22]. Additional types of, and steps in product-related selection, specification and negotiation that the customer is led into after his search are determined by a

---

18 Nenninger; M., Lawrenz; O., B2B-Erfolg durch eMarkets und eProcurement, 2002, P. 78.
19 Cf: Kollmann; T., E-Business, 2019, P. 547.
20 Cf: Schütt; M., Informationsmanagement auf elektronischen B2B-Marktplätzen, 2006, P. 97.
21 Cf: Prof. Dr. Schmid; B., Elektronische Märkte - Merkmale, Organisation und Potentiale, 2018, P. 21.
22 Cf: Teuteberg; F., E-Marketplace-Modelle, 2019, P. 4.

so-called matching-model that is applied by the e-marketplace provider on his trading platform[23]. Product and exchange related conditions can consist of multiple attributes such as: determination on terms of delivery, selection of product attributes such as color and size, pricing conditions and models[24]. It is crucial that all negotiations between customer and provider on the aspects mentioned above are both transparent (to both parties) as well as safe since any deviation from the terms of the contract would invalidate it[25]. Since, based on the applied e-matching model, the course of the process can be divided into three possible types of supplier/demander interaction, individual explanation will follow.

2.2.1. Online-Catalog-Process

The online-catalog-process is a variant from the numerous selection of matching models and describes a matching process in which the customer is given a selection of products with static product characteristics and a fixed price[26]. While fixed product- and pricing attributes such as color, size or delivery conditions (defined by the traders and marketplace operators) can be selected, advanced negotiations between provider and demander on a level of dynamic pricing (e.g. auctions) are not possible[27]:

Figure 5. Selection of Fixed Pricing- and Product Variants on a Single Catalog-Offer.

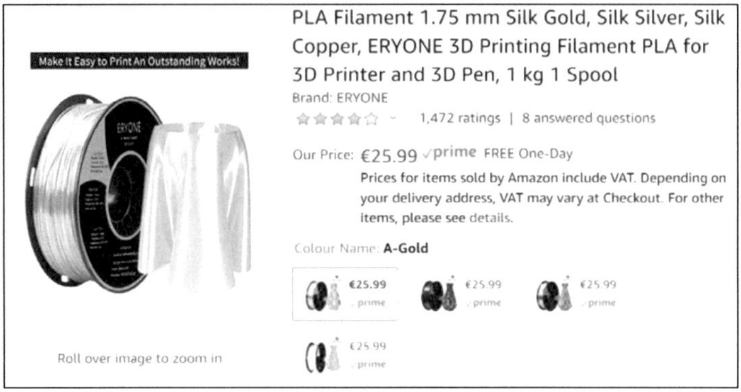

Source: Self-made screenshot from the website www.amazon.de.

---

23 Cf: Kollmann; T., E-Business, 2019, P. 548.
24 Cf: Kollmann; T., E-Business, 2019, P. 547.
25 Cf: Prof. Dr. Schmid; B., Elektronische Märkte - Merkmale, Organisation und Potentiale, 2018, P. 20.
26 Cf: Kollmann; T., E-Business, 2019, P. 548.
27 Cf: Schütt; M., Informationsmanagement auf elektronischen B2B-Marktplätzen, 2006, P. 99.

A clear advantage of an online catalog-based matching is the reduction of ambiguities as well as vague price and product conditions, since all contract-relevant data about the buyer and his offer are comprehensible in the offer description (Figure 5.).

2.2.2. Online-Request-Process

Another method of matching demander- and supplier-requests could be established through the online-request-process. The Marketplace itself acts as a third party and links specific product- or service-based customer requests – as a so called "Requests for Proposal"[28] - with fitting offers by certain providers[29]. One of the main differences compared to the online-catalog-process is that product- and price-specifications are not static and can be influenced on both sides by enquirer and supplier through negotiations[30]. An example of an e-marketplace that functions on a request based matching model would be the American listing-platform Craigslist:

Figure 6. The Broad Selection of Services and Products on Craigslist.

Source: Self-made screenshot from the website www.craigslist.org.

The above example of Craigslist illustrates an online-request process-based meeting of supplier and buyer. The website acts only as a mediator and matches a specific customer request with existing offers of the suppliers. Further exchange between both parties about, for example, discount requests and product adaptations can take place without any problems after the matching. However, as soon as a purchase contract is concluded, it will run through the e-marketplace provider (in this case Craigslist) itself.

---

28 Kollmann; T., E-Business, 2019, P. 549.
29 Cf: Kollmann; T., E-Business, 2019, PP. 549-550.
30 Cf: Kollmann; T., E-Business, 2019, P. 549.

2.2.3. Online-Auction-Process

The online auction process is yet another derivate of the electronic matching models that base on an existing product catalog[31]. The main difference compared to other matching models however lies in the transactional mechanism. Demanders are now able to participate in virtual auctions in which multiple demanders place their estimation of a suitable price for the given product/service. Based on the positioning of buyers and sellers, a separation is made between two different types of auctions[32]:

2.2.3.1. The Forward-Auction

The most common form of auction is the so called forward-auction in which many buyers place bids on a single offer[33]. Variants in which the price increases over the course of the auction are the "English and Yankee auctions"[34]. The opposing development of auctions in which the price is constantly lowering per bid are the "Dutch and free-fall auctions"[35]. The choice of any of the above models may be influenced by liquidity- or sales-based strategies by the marketplace operators[36].

2.2.3.2. The Reverse-Auction

The reverse-auction acts as the exact opposite of the forward-auction as the providers are now the instance that is bidding on a product that a certain customer wants to buy[37]:

31 Cf: Turban; E., Outland; J., King; D,. Lee; J. K., Liang; T-P., Turban; D., Electronic Commerce 2018, 2018, P. 55.
32 Cf: Turban; E., Outland; J., King; D,. Lee; J. K., Liang; T-P., Turban; D., Electronic Commerce 2018, 2018, P. 55.
33 Cf: Turban; E., Outland; J., King; D,. Lee; J. K., Liang; T-P., Turban; D., Electronic Commerce 2018, 2018, P. 55.
34 Turban; E., Outland; J., King; D,. Lee; J. K., Liang; T-P., Turban; D., Electronic Commerce 2018, 2018, P. 55.
35 Turban; E., Outland; J., King; D,. Lee; J. K., Liang; T-P., Turban; D., Electronic Commerce 2018, 2018, P. 55.
36 Cf: Kollmann; T., E-Business, 2019, P. 551.
37 Cf: Turban; E., Outland; J., King; D,. Lee; J. K., Liang; T-P., Turban; D., Electronic Commerce 2018, 2018, P. 55.

Figure 7. Reverse Auction: Providers are Lowering the Price.

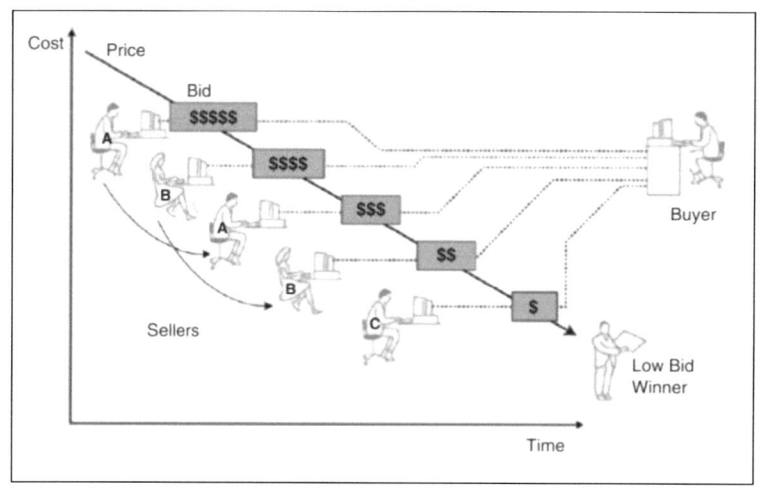

Source: Turban; E., Outland; J., King; D,. Lee; J. K., Liang; T-P., Turban; D., Electronic Commerce 2018, 2018, P. 56.

As can be seen in figure 7. the product-price is gradually lowering by each placed bid by the providers. The lowest bid wins the auction and thereby the sale with the customer.

2.3. Phase 3: Completing the Transaction – The E-Transaction Process

As soon as all negotiations about price and product features have been completed and the product has been saved in an "electronic shopping cart"[38], taking into account the delivery conditions, only the payment via the e-transaction process remains. As soon as the transaction has been verified, through the e-transaction-process, the e-markteplace receives confirmation that the delivery can be approved and the legal contract between buyer, seller and e-marketplace provider is finally closed[39].As indicated in the introduction above, the e-transaction process accompanies the actual acceptance of payment and the related transfer of the contractual ownership of the product to the buyer[40]. It also assists with the accounting settlements on the part of the provider and the platform operator to make the completed transaction verifiable[41]. Depending on the structure of the e-marketplace, this process can be partially or full automated. It is also often the case that external payment-tool-providers are involved in order to expand the

38 Turban; E., Outland; J., King; D,. Lee; J. K., Liang; T-P., Turban; D., Electronic Commerce 2018, 2018, P. 53.
39 Cf: Deges; F., Grundlagen des E-Commerce, 2020, P. 187.
40 Cf: Teuteberg; F., E-Marketplace-Modelle, 2019, P. 4.
41 Cf: Kollmann; T., E-Business, 2019, PP. 555-556.

range of possible payment options and to outsource the actual process of verifying incoming payments[42]:

Figure 8. User View of the Payment Process on Amazon.

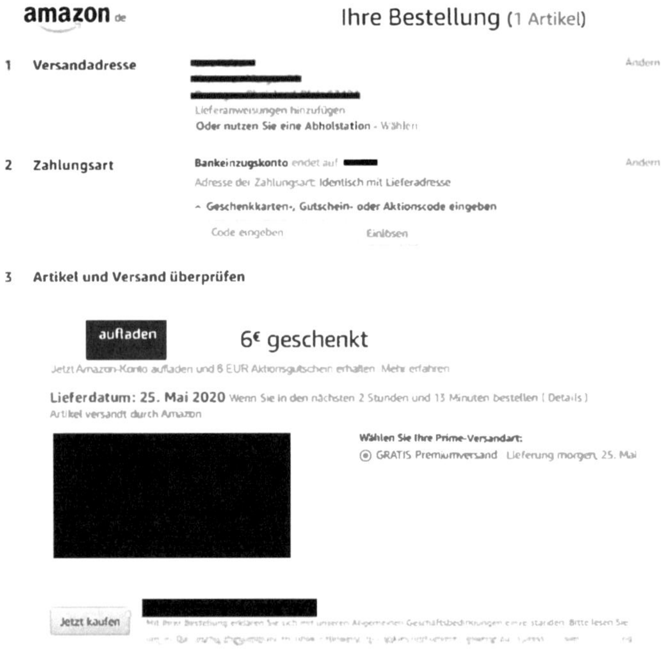

Source: Self-made screenshot from the website www.amazon.de.

As can be seen in the figure above, the e-transaction process takes place shortly before the completion of the order. A suitable means of payment is agreed upon and the user gets the last chance to check all order-specific details. After the buyer clicks on "Jetzt Kaufen" and virtually signs all the contractual details, the e-marketplace checks the receipt of payment and the order can be released.

2.4. Phase 4: After Sales Service – The After-e-Sales Process

Although the transaction has now been completed, the interaction between customer and marketplace usually does not end here. Customers may be unhappy with their order and request a return or, on the contrary, may be willing to make a new purchase[43]. In either case, follow-up customer care is essential.

---

42 Cf: Turban; E., Outland; J., King; D., Lee; J. K., Liang; T-P., Turban; D., Electronic Commerce 2018, 2018, P. 108.

43 Cf: Teuteberg; F., E-Marketplace-Modelle. 2019. P. 4.

Based on the customers satisfaction with the product, the after-e-sales process can be divided into two separate core areas: returns-management and repurchase-service[44] [45] [46]:

Figure 9. The two Possible Routes of the After-e-Sales Process.

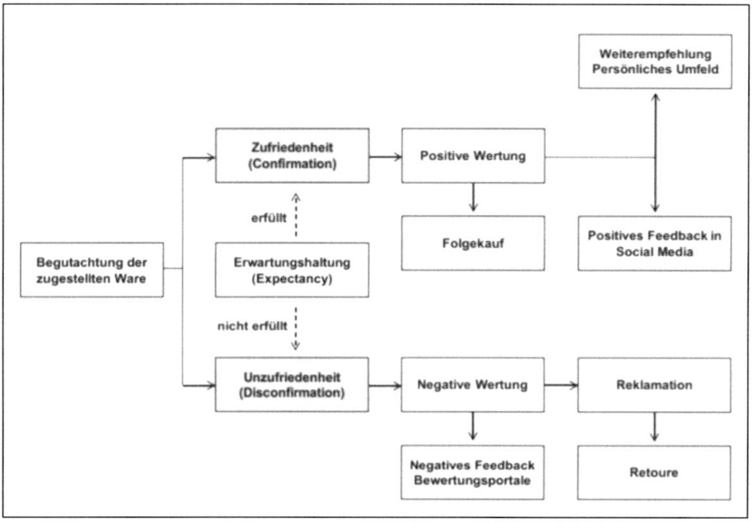

Source: Deges; F., Grundlagen des E-Commerce, 2020, P. 198.

2.4.1. Returns-Management

Reasons for the return shipment of ordered goods can in most cases be assigned to four decisive categories: price-, product-, customer- and logistics-related reasons[47]. For legal reasons it is also essential to have a fully functional returns management system that checks and validates incoming returns requests and subsequently books and initiates them in a communicative manner with the customer[48].

---

44 Cf: Kollmann; T., E-Business, 2019, PP. 558-559.
45 CF: Köcher; M., Fulfillment im Electronic Commerce, 2006, PP. 15-17.
46 Cf: Deges; F., Grundlagen des E-Commerce, 2020, PP. 187-189.
47 Cf: Deges; F., Grundlagen des E-Commerce, 2020, P. 198-199.
48 CF: Köcher; M., Fulfillment im Electronic Commerce, 2006, PP. 16-19.

2.4.2. Repurchase-Service

Köcher defines the repurchase service as an accompanying process which the customer undertakes after his order in the form of: product advice[49], product support, repair services and further purchase recommendations[50]. On e-marketplaces, this can be recognized, among other things, by product-relevant insertions and links which should entice the customer to be accompanied in his product use on the one hand and on the other hand to stimulate the re-purchase of the same or similar products.

3. Conclusion

Summarizing the results, it is clear that the e-fulfillment process could become more and more nested in its by definition very comprehensive meaning. However, it is also noticeable how essential the existence and smooth exchange of the individual sub-processes is for a functioning e-marketplace. The results of the research clearly show that the first phases of the e-fulfillment process in particular are essential for customer acquisition and retention. However, it can also be seen that there is still a high potential for improvement and expansion in the individual sub-processes (above all in the after-sales processes), which will presumably be exploited in the future due to the increasing demands of customers.

---

49 Cf: Große Holforth; D., Schlüsselfaktoren im E-Commerce, 2017, PP. 29-30.
50 Cf: Köcher; M., Fulfillment im Electronic Commerce, 2006, P. 15.

Bibliography

Deges, Frank (Grundlagen des E-Commerce, 2020): Grundlagen des E-Commerce, Wiesbaden: Springer Gabler, 2020

Große Holtforth, Dominik (Innovationen, Skaleneffekte, Daten und Kundenzentrierung, 2017): Schlüsselfaktoren im E-Commerce - Innovationen, Skaleneffekte, Daten und Kundenzentrierung, Wiesbaden: Springer Gabler, 2017

Köcher, Martin-Matthias (Gestaltungsansätze, Determinanten, Wirkungen, 2006): Fulfillment im Electronic Commerce - Gestaltungsansätze, Determinanten, Wirkungen, Wiesbaden: Deutscher Universitats-Verlag I GWV Fachverlage GmbH, 2006

Kollmann, Tobias (Grundlagen elektronischer Geschäftsprozesse in der Digitalen Wirtschaft, 2019): E-Business - Grundlagen elektronischer Geschäftsprozesse in der Digitalen Wirtschaft, 7. Aufl., Wiesbaden: Springer Gabler, 2019

Mufatto, Moreno, Payaro, Andrea (A comparison of cases in the motorcycle industry, 2004): Implementation of e-procurement and e-fulfillment processes: A comparison of cases in the motorcycle industry, Padua/Italy: DIMEG, University of Padua, 2004

Nenninger, Michael, Lawrenz, Oliver (Strategien und Konzepte, Systeme und Architekturen, Erfahrungen und Best Practice, 2002): B2B-Erfolg durch eMarkets und eProcurement - Strategien und Konzepte, Systeme und Architekturen, Erfahrungen und Best Practice, 2. Aufl., Brauchschweig/Wiesbaden: Friedr. Vieweg & Sohn Verlagsgesellschaft mbH, 2002

Olbrich, Rainer, Schultz, Carsten D., Holsing, Christian (Ein einführendes Lehr- und Übungsbuch, 2019): Electronic Commerce und Online-Marketing Ein einführendes Lehr- und Übungsbuch, 2. Aufl., Berlin: Springer Gabler, 2019

Schmid, Prof. Dr. Beat F. (Merkmale, Organisation und Potentiale, 2018): Elektronische Märkte - Merkmale, Organisation und Potentiale, St. Gallen/Switzerland: The NetAcademy, 2018

Schütt, Michaela (Unterstützung der elektronischen Beschaffung durch integrierte Informationsprozesse, 2006): Informationsmanagement auf elektronischen B2B-Marktplätzen - Unterstützung der elektronischen Beschaffung durch integrierte Informationsprozesse, Wiesbaden: Deutscher Universitats-Verlag I GWV Fachverlage GmbH , 2006

Schütte, Reinhard (E-Fulfillment, 2018): E-Fulfillment, Wiesbaden: Springer Fachmedien Wiesbaden GmbH, 2018

Teuteberg, Frank (E-Marketplace-Modelle, 2019): E-Marketplace-Modelle, Wiesbaden Springer Fachmedien Wiesbaden GmbH, ein Teil von Springer Nature, 2019

V

Turban, Efraim, Outland, John, King, David, Lee, Jae Kyu, Liang, Ting-Peng, Turban, Deborrah C. (A Managerial and Social Networks Perspective, 2018) Electronic Commerce 2018, 9. Aufl., Cham, Switzerland: Springer Nature, 2018

Turban, Efraim, Whiteside, Judy, King, David, Outland, Jon (Introduction to Electronic Commerce and Social Commerce, 2017) Introduction to Electronic Commerce and Social Commerce, Cham/Switzerland: Springer Nature Switzerland AG, 2017

Wirtz, Bernd W. (Concepts, Models, and the Alphabet Case Study, 2019) Digital Business Models - Concepts, Models, and the Alphabet Case Study, Cham/Switzerland: Springer Nature Switzerland AG, 2019